GREATEST MOMENTS
IN WOMEN'S
SPORTS

BY TODD KORTEMEIER

WOMEN IN
SPORTS

SportsZone

An Imprint of Abdo Publishing
abdopublishing.com

abdopublishing.com

Published by Abdo Publishing, a division of ABDO, PO Box 398166, Minneapolis,
Minnesota 55439. Copyright © 2018 by Abdo Consulting Group, Inc. International
copyrights reserved in all countries. No part of this book may be reproduced in any form
without written permission from the publisher. SportsZone™ is a trademark and logo of
Abdo Publishing.

Printed in the United States of America, North Mankato, Minnesota
042017
092017

Cover Photo: Michael Caulfield/AP Images
Interior Photos: Michael Caulfield/AP Images, 1; Bettmann/Getty Images, 5; AP Images,
6, 9, 10–11; Jerry Cooke/Sports Illustrated/Getty Images, 12; AFP/Getty Images, 14; Eric
Risberg/AP Images, 16–17; Lennox McLendon/AP Images, 18–19; Dieter Endlicher/AP
Images, 20; Elsa/Getty Images Sport/Getty Images, 22–23; Mark J. Terrill/AP Images, 25;
Lacy Atkins/The San Francisco Examiner/AP Images, 26; Michael Conroy/AP Images, 28–
29, 32; Zach Bolinger/Icon Sportswire, 30; Michael S. Wirtz/The Philadelphia Enquirer/AP
Images, 34–35; Gene J. Puskar/AP Images, 36; Sean Simmers/PennLive.com/AP Images,
39; Al Bello/Getty Images Sport/Getty Images, 40–41; Lee Jin-man/AP Images, 42; Kyodo/
AP Images, 45

Editor: Patrick Donnelly
Series Designer: Laura Polzin
Content Consultant: Rita Liberti, PhD, Professor of Kinesiology, California State
    University, East Bay

Publisher's Cataloging-in-Publication Data

Names: Kortemeier, Todd, author.
Title: Greatest moments in women's sports / by Todd Kortemeier.
Description: Minneapolis, MN : Abdo Publishing, 2018. | Series: Women in
    sports | Includes bibliographical references and index.
Identifiers: LCCN 2016962126 | ISBN 9781532111556 (lib. bdg.) |
    ISBN 9781680789409 (ebook)
Subjects: LCSH: Athletes--Juvenile literature. | Women athletes--Juvenile
    literature. | Sports--Miscellanea--Juvenile literature.
Classification: DDC 796--dc23
LC record available at http://lccn.loc.gov/2016962126

TABLE OF
CONTENTS

EDERLE SWIMS THE CHANNEL

1

Gertrude Ederle stood on a beach in northern France in the early morning of August 6, 1926. The water was cold, but the seas were calm. The English coast lay 21 miles (33.8 kilometers) in the distance. This time, she was going to make it.

The 21-year-old New Yorker's first attempt to swim across the English Channel ended in failure. Her coach feared for her safety and made her quit after nearly nine hours in the water. She fired that coach and hired one who had experience swimming the Channel himself. Together, a year later, they would conquer it.

The English Channel is an incredibly difficult swim. The water is cold, even in the summer. Strong winds often kick up waves several feet high. Even for experienced swimmers, it's a major challenge. At the time of Ederle's swim, only five people had ever made it across. And all of them were men.

Gertrude Ederle gets greased up to protect her skin during her English Channel crossing.

EDERLE'S DEAFNESS

Ederle had trouble hearing dating back to her childhood. After her channel swim, she became a swimming instructor, but by 1945 she was totally deaf. Instead of letting that slow her down, she used her deafness in a positive way, becoming a swimming instructor for deaf children. She never learned sign language, but she showed children they could be comfortable in the water without hearing.

Ederle started her swim at 7:08 a.m. The seas were calm at first. But she ran into trouble at noon as storms significantly slowed her progress. Another storm hit at 6:00 p.m., and her coach suggested she quit. But Ederle's family was also in the boat following her, and they encouraged her to keep going. Her father had promised her a new car if she completed the journey. To motivate his daughter, he called out to her, reminding her of the prize that awaited.

Ederle pushed through more rough seas and reached Kingsdown, England, at 9:04 p.m. The straight-line trip of 21 miles (33.8 km) had become 35 miles (56.3 km) with the waves pushing her off course. But she didn't care. Her time

Ederle faced difficult conditions in the water during her swim.

of 14 hours, 31 minutes had shattered the previous record by two hours.

A hero's welcome awaited Ederle upon her return to the United States. She was honored with a parade in New York City. Songs were written for her. She even got to meet President Calvin Coolidge at the White House. But after the excitement died down, her life returned to a quiet pace. Athletes—especially female athletes—in the 1920s did not earn the life-changing money that top athletes make today. Ederle lived a humble life near New York City, occasionally giving interviews on anniversaries of her famous swim.

Ederle was already an accomplished swimmer by the time of her Channel swim. She won a gold and two bronze medals at the 1924 Olympics. She set 29 world and national records between 1921 and 1925. Ederle was inducted into the International Swimming Hall of Fame in 1965.

Ederle died in 2003 at the age of 93. In the years since her feat, many women have taken up the challenge of the English Channel. Nearly 600 had completed it by the end of 2016.

Ederle was an Olympic champion before she swam the English Channel.

CHAPTER 2

PERFECTION IN MONTREAL

Nadia Comăneci didn't really see what the big deal was. The 14-year-old Romanian gymnast was used to nailing her routines in practice. Her performance at the 1976 Summer Olympics in Montreal, Canada, didn't feel all that different to her. But she soon realized that she'd changed gymnastics forever.

Nadia had been a gymnast since the age of 6. By the time she was 13, she was one of the best in the world. She won gold in all but one event at the 1975 European Championships. Expectations were high when Nadia stepped onto the mat in Montreal.

She was the last to perform on the uneven bars for Team Romania. Nadia whipped her body around the bars, executing all of the moves in her routine. She thought her performance went well, and she began thinking about the next event while waiting for her score. A roar from the crowd snapped her back to the present, and she took a look at the scoreboard.

Nadia Comăneci tumbled her way into the hearts of Olympic fans in 1976.

Nadia performs on the uneven bars in Montreal.

She expected to see a good score, so the 1.00 on display confused her. But she didn't earn a 1.0. She had scored a perfect 10. The scoreboard wasn't built to handle a perfect score. It only had room for one digit before the decimal point. The International Olympic Committee hadn't considered the possibility that a gymnast would achieve perfection.

But not only was it possible, it became normal for Nadia. She achieved six more perfect 10s in Montreal that year. She won five medals, including gold in the all-around, balance beam, and uneven bars. Her release move from the uneven bars wowed the gymnastics world. Gymnasts today call the move the Comăneci salto.

NADIA IN 1980

Comăneci returned to Olympic competition in 1980 in Moscow, Russia. She won four medals in those Games, including two gold. But one of her silver medals was controversial. Comăneci lost a very close decision in the all-around individual competition to Yelena Davydova of the Soviet Union. Romanian officials protested the decision, believing that hometown judges rigged the scores in Davydova's favor.

Nadia celebrates next to the scoreboard that couldn't properly display her perfect score.

After the Olympics, it was clear that Nadia was the best gymnast in the world. But her contribution to the sport became so much bigger than that. Her athleticism had rarely been seen before in women's gymnastics. Though she had a tiny frame, she was incredibly strong and could pull off skills that only men had done at the time.

The popularity of gymnastics exploded, especially with young girls. The sport became faster and more exciting than ever. Comăneci was the role model for any girl looking to get started in gymnastics. In 1989, she moved to the United States and became an American citizen. She married fellow gymnast Bart Conner in 1996. The two run a gymnastics academy in Oklahoma.

Due to a change in 2006, gymnasts are now given two scores, one for difficulty and one for execution. There is no longer a maximum, "perfect" score. Scores for good routines typically range from 15 to 16 points.

FAMILY AFFAIR IN SEOUL

The 1988 Summer Olympics in Seoul, South Korea, were a family affair for two American stars who set records that have stood the test of time.

Florence Griffith burst onto the scene at the 1984 Summer Games in Los Angeles. She won silver in the 200-meter dash, but she took gold in the eyes of her fans, who loved her flashy outfits and her uniquely painted fingernails. After she married fellow Olympian Al Joyner, she changed her name to Florence Griffith Joyner and became known simply as "Flo-Jo."

At the 1988 Olympic trials, Griffith Joyner smashed the world record in the 100-meter dash. Her time of 10.49 seconds beat the old mark by three tenths of a second. It was faster than the men's record in many countries. Then in Seoul, Flo-Jo broke the Olympic record in the 100 and set a new world record in the 200. She earned another gold medal in the 4×100 relay and a silver in the 4×400.

Florence Griffith Joyner celebrates her victory in the 100-meter dash at the 1988 Summer Olympics.

Jackie Joyner-Kersee grimaces during her shot put toss at the heptathlon competition in Seoul.

Through 2016, her world records still stand and are among the longest-lasting world records in the sport.

Meanwhile, Al Joyner had a sister who was pretty special in her own right. Jackie Joyner was born on

March 3, 1962. She was named in honor of Jackie Kennedy, First Lady of the United States at the time. Joyner's grandmother came up with the idea, believing that baby Jackie would one day be the first lady of something.

It turned out the she became the greatest athlete in the world. Joyner, who married her coach, Bob Kersee, competed in several track and field events, but she became known for her performance in the heptathlon. The heptathlon is a collection of seven events that test different types of skills. Athletes receive points based on their performance in each event.

THE LOSS OF FLO-JO

On September 21, 1998, Griffith Joyner died in her sleep at the age of 38. She had suffered from seizures previously, with no known cause. Her autopsy revealed that she had a weakness of blood vessels in her brain that had gone undetected. In 2000 a public park in her hometown of Mission Viejo, California, was named in her honor.

Joyner-Kersee lost the 1984 Olympic heptathlon by just five points, an agonizingly small margin in a sport where scores routinely top 6,000 points. But after that narrow defeat, she won the heptathlon at her next nine meets. At the 1986 Goodwill Games, Joyner-Kersee became the first woman to surpass 7,000 points in the heptathlon.

Sports Illustrated **published a list of the top female athletes of the 20th century. Jackie Joyner-Kersee took the top spot, and Florence Griffith Joyner came in at 11.**

By the 1988 Olympics, she was a major favorite, and she didn't disappoint. Joyner-Kersee broke her own world record for the fourth time, finishing with 7,291 points. But she wasn't done. She added a gold medal in the long jump five days later.

Joyner-Kersee's world record in the heptathlon remained standing through 2016. She also had the six best scores of all time. Few other women can make such a strong claim to the title of best athlete of all time.

Griffith Joyner, *left*, embraces US track legend Wilma Rudolph.

CHASTAIN CLINCHES THE CUP

With the Women's World Cup championship at her feet, Brandi Chastain lined up the most important kick in the history of women's soccer. The United States and China had just played 120 minutes without either side scoring. The 1999 Women's World Cup would be decided by penalty kicks.

The teams took turns shooting. China scored on four of its five shots. But the United States had converted its first four penalty kicks. That meant that if the last American player came through, the United States would win the title.

Chastain wasn't supposed to be in that spot. She originally was listed sixth on the list of US shooters.

Tension shows on the faces of members of the US team as they watch Brandi Chastain line up her penalty kick against China.

She had missed against China four months earlier. She then changed her technique to use her left foot, which kept goalkeepers guessing.

Just before the Women's World Cup final shootout, US coach Tony DiCicco moved Chastain to fifth. That move put her in position to clinch the championship. Though she was exhausted from the match, Chastain was focused and ready to kick. The crowd of 90,000 at the Rose Bowl in Pasadena, California, went quiet.

Chastain took her run up and struck it with her left foot. She watched it spin toward the goal, perfectly placed. China's keeper, Gao Hong, made a desperate dive to her left, but the ball settled into the top corner of the net. In her excitement, Chastain whipped off her jersey

THE USWNT

Since playing its first match in 1985, the US Women's National Team (USWNT) has been one of the best in women's soccer. The US women have never finished lower than third at the Women's World Cup and have won three titles. They have won four Olympic gold medals. No other country can match that.

Gao Hong can't reach Chastain's shot as it slips just inside the post to give the United States the Women's World Cup championship.

and swung it over her head. Her teammates mobbed her in front of the goal as the United States celebrated another Women's World Cup title.

Like many American girls, Chastain did not grow up having a Women's World Cup to watch. Eight years earlier, she'd played in the first one ever. The 1999 Women's World Cup was the first played in the United States, and Chastain

and her teammates won over fans from coast to coast. Thanks to their heroics, the Women's World Cup became a major event in the world of sports.

Chastain now coaches girls' soccer and says she's had many players who weren't born or were too young to remember her historic

Chastain set the record for most goals in a USWNT match with five on April 18, 1991, against Mexico. Six other US women have since tied the record.

goal. That 1999 title was the most recent for the United States until 2015. Then a new generation of US stars beat Japan for the country's third Women's World Cup title. Some of the US players remembered clearly where they were when Chastain scored. Abby Wambach, the leading goal scorer in the history of US women's soccer, was in college. Forward Sydney Leroux was 9 years old and living in Canada. Her mother is Canadian but her father is American, so she could play for either country. She says that Chastain's goal convinced her to play for the United States.

A relieved and exultant Chastain rejoices after her game-winning shot.

NEARLY PERFECT

When the University of Connecticut (UConn) women's basketball team cut down the nets as national champions on April 5, 2016, it continued a remarkable run. But it was the end of the line for perhaps the best player in school history.

It was fitting that Breanna Stewart starred as UConn won its fourth straight national title. She led the Huskies with 24 points, 10 rebounds, and six assists as UConn crushed Syracuse 82–51.

Every championship is special. But winning had become routine for Stewart and the Huskies. From the time Stewart arrived at UConn in 2012, the Huskies went an astounding 151–5. Four of those losses came during her freshman year. They won the national title in each of her four seasons. It was the greatest four-year run in the history of Division I women's college basketball.

Stewart came into college basketball facing high expectations. She had been named national player of

Breanna Stewart's swarming defense played a big role in UConn's success.

GOING PRO

With her achievements in college, Stewart was expected to be in demand as a pro. She was taken first overall in the 2016 Women's National Basketball Association (WNBA) draft by the Seattle Storm. Two of her UConn teammates, Moriah Jefferson and Morgan Tuck, were the next two picks. Stewart won the 2016 Rookie of the Year Award after leading all first-year players in points, rebounds, and blocked shots.

the year by several organizations while playing at Cicero North High School in upstate New York. Stewart began exceeding those expectations the moment she arrived in Connecticut. The 6-foot, 4-inch forward was a strong post player on both sides of the ball. Her shot blocking and rebounding keyed the Huskies defense. And her passing and shooting created more space on the floor. That allowed her more room in the post on offense.

After winning three straight NCAA titles—and being named Most Outstanding Player of the Final Four in each—Stewart set her sights on a new goal. UConn had won three straight national titles from 2002 through

Stewart's all-around offensive game made her a threat anywhere on the court.

From left, Stewart, Moriah Jefferson, and Morgan Tuck celebrate with the national championship trophy in 2016.

2004. But the most dominant program in women's college basketball had never won four in a row.

Stewart simply put the team on her back during her senior season. The Huskies went 38–0, their second undefeated season in three years. Stewart won her third straight national player of the year award. And she was the Final Four's Most Outstanding Player for an unprecedented fourth straight year.

After her first WNBA season, Stewart signed with a team in China. She played for Shanghai during the WNBA offseason. She was averaging 31.4 points per game when she injured her knee and had to return to the United States to rest and recover.

Stewart left college with the Huskies riding a 75-game winning streak. Her former teammates carried on the tradition the next season. They snapped the NCAA record set when UConn won 90 straight games from 2008 to 2010. The Huskies' streak eventually reached 111 games before Mississippi State shocked them with an overtime defeat in the NCAA semifinals on March 31, 2017.

CHAPTER 6

MO'NE THROWS HEAT

Mo'Ne Davis is used to surprising people. When she was just 7 years old, a youth basketball coach in her hometown near Philadelphia spotted her throwing a football with some friends. The little girl could throw a perfect spiral. That coach, Steve Bandura, asked her to be on his basketball team.

He warned her that it was an all-boys team. But Mo'Ne didn't care. She showed up at practice two days later and jumped right into drills like she'd been playing the sport for years. Mo'Ne was similarly gifted when it came to baseball. She played at a high level right away, joining a south Philadelphia traveling team by the age of 7. She drew crowds who came to see her strike out batter after batter. Mo'Ne didn't use trick pitches to fool hitters. She blew them away with a fastball that reached 70 miles per hour (112.7 kmh).

When she was 13, Mo'Ne and her teammates won the Mid-Atlantic Little League championship and a trip to

Mo'Ne Davis pitches in the Pennsylvania state Little League championship game in 2014.

MO'NE'S OTHER LOVE

Despite her success in baseball, Mo'Ne's favorite sport is basketball. Her dream is to play college basketball at the University of Connecticut and then play in the WNBA. She started at point guard for her high school varsity team when she was a freshman.

the 2014 Little League World Series (LLWS). She was their star pitcher. At the regional tournament, she struck out 17 batters in 12 2/3 innings. A girl playing in the LLWS was rare, but not new. She was the 18th in history and the sixth from the United States.

A lot of young pitchers have trouble throwing strikes. It can be even more difficult in the tense atmosphere at the LLWS. Pitching on national television in front of a big crowd can be intimidating. But Mo'Ne didn't seem to notice. In her first start, she allowed just two hits and struck out eight in a 4–0 win. She became a fan favorite as huge crowds turned out to watch her pitch. Mo'Ne even was featured on the cover of *Sports Illustrated*.

Mo'Ne signs autographs at the 2014 Little League World Series.

In her next start, Mo'Ne struck out six batters in 2 1/3 innings. But her team lost to Nevada 8–1. They were eliminated from the LLWS with an ensuing loss to Chicago. But as the first girl to win a LLWS game, Davis would not be soon forgotten.

Mo'Ne was the first Little League World Series player, boy or girl, to be featured on the cover of *Sports Illustrated*.

A young fan shows her support for Mo'Ne at the LLWS.

LEDECKY
MAKES A SPLASH

When Katie Ledecky was nine years old, she met swimming legend Michael Phelps. Katie was a swimmer herself, so she was thrilled to meet one of the best in the sport's history. She even got a photo of Phelps signing an autograph for her.

Ten years later, the two re-created the photo. Only this time, Phelps was the fan getting the autograph. Ledecky had just finished the 2016 Olympics as one of the most decorated swimmers in US history.

Like Phelps, Ledecky grew up in Maryland. She started swimming at age 6 with her older brother, who also was a swimmer. Her mother was a swimmer in college at the University of New Mexico. Katie quickly became an elite distance swimmer and qualified for the 2012 Olympics in London, England, when she was just 15 years old.

Katie Ledecky reacts after winning the 800-meter freestyle gold medal at the 2012 Olympic Games in London.

But that was only the beginning. In preparing for the 2016 Games in Rio de Janeiro, Brazil, Ledecky focused beyond

Ledecky is unmatched when it comes to the 800-meter freestyle. She has beaten her own world record in the event six times.

the 800-meter freestyle. After all, the 800 was her best event, and she already held the world record. She would swim the 200, 400, and 800 in Rio, plus two relay races. The 800 was easy. She crushed her own world record by two whole seconds. She did similarly in the 400 and beat the current world record holder in the 200. She was the first woman to win all three of those races since 1968.

In the 4×200 relay, four swimmers each swim 200 meters. When Ledecky took over to swim her part, her team was .89 seconds behind. By the time Ledecky was done, they led by 1.84 seconds. It was another gold.

Her fifth event was the 4×100 relay. It was shorter than Ledecky was used to swimming, but she performed well. She did her best to make up a .42-second deficit, but she couldn't quite catch gold medal winners from Australia. The US team had to settle for a silver, but that made five total Olympic medals for Ledecky. She was only the third

Ledecky continued her dominance in Rio.

LEDECKY'S 2012 OLYMPICS

As a high school sophomore in 2012, Katie was the youngest member of Team USA. She nonetheless qualified for the final of the 800-meter freestyle, her only event at the Olympics. Katie took the lead on the first of eight laps. She fell behind on the second lap, then regained the lead on the third. From there she kept it for good and won gold. She finished well ahead of the field with a time of 8:14.63, beating the US record held by Janet Evans.

woman from the United States to win four gold medals at one Olympics.

But Ledecky was far from done. Though a college career at Stanford University awaited her next, she was already looking forward to swimming in Tokyo, Japan, for the 2020 Olympics.

Ledecky shows off her gold medal after defending her title in the 800 freestyle.

GLOSSARY

CHANNEL
A narrow body of water between two land masses.

DRAFT
A system that allows teams to acquire new players coming into a league.

FAVORITE
The person or team that is expected to win.

FREESTYLE
A competition in which swimmers may use any stroke of their choice.

HEPTATHLON
A competition in track and field in which each participant takes part in the same seven events.

PENALTY KICK
A free kick at the goal, defended only by the keeper, awarded after a foul in the penalty area; also used to break ties in a shootout.

POINT GUARD
A position in basketball that usually directs a team's offense.

RELAY
A race between teams made up of several participants who compete one at a time.

ROUTINE
A fixed sequence of actions designed to demonstrate a gymnast's skills on a particular apparatus.

SOPHOMORE
A second-year student.

UNEVEN BARS
A gymnastics competition performed between two bars of uneven height.

BOOKS

Davis, Mo'Ne. *Remember My Name: My Story from First Pitch to Game Changer.* New York: Harper, 2015.

Kawa, Katie. *Women in Sports.* New York: PowerKids Press, 2016.

Rutherford, Kristina. *Level the Playing Field: The Past, Present, and Future of Women's Pro Sports.* Berkeley, CA: Owlkids Books, 2016.

Trusdell, Brian. *US Women Win the World Cup.* Minneapolis, MN: Abdo Publishing, 2015.

WEBSITES

To learn more about women in sports, visit **abdobooklinks.com**. These links are routinely monitored and updated to provide the most current information available.

PLACE TO VISIT

Women's Basketball Hall of Fame
700 South Hall of Fame Drive
Knoxville, Tennessee 37915
865–633–9000
www.wbhof.com
The Women's Basketball Hall of Fame is the only one of its kind. It showcases the greatest players and people from the history of women's basketball. It also includes areas where fans can test their basketball skills or see the world's largest basketball.

INDEX

ABOUT THE AUTHOR

Todd Kortemeier is a writer and editor from Minneapolis. A graduate of the University of Minnesota's School of Journalism and Mass Communication, he has written more than 25 sports books for young people.